# GOLDEN POEMS FROM AFRICA

Michael K. Twum

**AFRAM PUBLICATIONS (GHANA) LIMITED**

**Published by:**

Afram Publications (Ghana) Ltd.,

P.O. Box M 18,

Accra, Ghana

**Revised edition, 2000**

**ISBN:** 9964 70 224 8

Printed by:

To all the self-pitying ones,
To the afflicted
And to all those who have
Lost living hope


All men are brothers;
All women are sisters;
All men and women
Are brothers and sisters

## CONTENTS

Preface

## PREFACE

This book is not only for Africans, though written in Africa. It is intended for everyone - mostly for those who are confused about the condition the world is in, for those who are concerned for a more stable world, for all peace-loving people.

Readers may find in these poems some convincing arguments that people of the world have almost all the same problems, problems created by themselves.

This book is to help identify such problems and provide some help in better understanding such problems and difficulties.

I am not a prophet, but I do have the desire to communicate my analyses of human activities, of confrontations with different sorts of people, of special characters I have met. It is this desire that brought about this work, which I think is suitable for our era.

Golden Poems from Africa **is written in clear and simple English to enable even the "enemies" of poetry to read these golden verses without any difficulty.**

Perfect poems for our times - for those living without hope.

**M.K.T.**

## FOR THE USE NOT THE BEAUTY

I am for the use
Not the beauty.
Food and water able to
Go through my mouth,
And speech able to come forth it,
That's enough
And not the thickness of my lips.

I want to live:
Breathing through my nose,
I am for the use
Not for the breadth of my nose.

I have a black head
Full of poems.
Taking my pen,
I wrote poems.

## THE PARADISE

There's sweet wind somewhere.
Where comes the slow beautiful music.
Birds of all colours chanting,
What do you take me to be?

Tall trees in beautiful sights,
Snaky rivers upon your surface.
Hills and mountains decorated to please,
A beautiful garden you are.

Red, yellow, green, smiling.
How welcomed are your flowers,
The blue sea giving its rich wind;
Nothing to match your beauty.

Animals roaming here and there.
In peace, the lion ate its herb.
Fruits aplenty high on trees.
Imagine such a park.

The rain watering it day and night.
All seem to be natural.
Dead leaves enriching your soil,
No work of a human being.

And freely man walked among the
Trees, not knowing he will ever die
Among the roses and the lilies,
And ate freely his nourishing fruits.

But the devil came
And the woman obeyed him.
Such a wicked act
Which made the paradise go away.

2

Will it ever come again?
I surely believe it.
Keep waiting for it
And you will see it again.

## THE GREATEST ARTIST

Who designed the solar system?
Who made the blue sky?
Who made the moon and sun?
Turn to the greatest Artist.

Who designed the ocean?
Who designed the trees?
Who designed the mountain?
Turn to the greatest Artist.

It is true of the greatest Artist:
He designed man, his head, feet,
Belly and hands.
Oh, what a marvelous gift we have.
Turn to the greatest Artist.

Hair in different colours,
Skins in different hues,
Eyes grasping in perfect colour,
Turn to the greatest Artist.

Different beasts in forest,
Beautiful birds in trees,
Flowers booming forth in quantity.
Turn to the greatest Artist.

Why not be content with how you are?
Why am I short, tall, fat or thin?
Why am I black, white, red or brown?
Turn to the greatest Artist.

And how do I know the greatest Artist?
It is simple: God is the greatest Artist.
He designed all things you see:
Turn to Him.

## TIME WAITS FOR NO MAN

Time waits for no man;
What you have to do, do it now,
For time waits no man.
Plan accordingly.

Do not say, "I will do it tomorrow."
Tomorrow is not there for you.
You may leave the world today.
So what you have to do, do it now.

You are waiting for time:
Good, it's good of you,
But time is not waiting for you.
And soon you will waste time.

If you see you are late,
Think of the time you wasted.
Never waste the time.
For the wasted time will never come again.

## ESPECIALLY FOR MEN

Who are you, man?
Do you say you are the opposite of woman?
If that is that,
Then you can be one.

If you are a being,
Then you must know this:
That the woman is not your slave;
She is also a fellow being.

If you are a married man
Why not be humble?
Loving your wife always,
You are the best of men.

But there's something stupid in man.
He keeps quarreling with his egg:
Do you forget it will break?
You are a bad man.

You are to love your wife.
You are to cherish her.
Meeting her early after work,
You are a super hushand.

You have been eating in your friend's house.
Oh, how wicked you are!
Your wife will he feeling unloved
And will find a new man.

Do you divorce your wife for her  barreness?
You are an imp.
Keep loving her.
For God's time is the best.

Do you help your wife in the kitchen?
Do not say, "It is not my duty."
It is part of your love,
You must know.

Talking always with your wife.
And discussing matters tête à tête.
Rendering her due unselfishly,
You are a real man.

## WE LIVE IN A WONDERFUL WORLD

We live in a wonderful world
Where all things are possible.
Free as this may be,
Thanks to its Maker.

A beautiful sun up high,
A glorious moon at night,
A forest full of good food,
All surrounded by a great sea.

Go out while it is still night
And contemplate the bright stars
In the clear blue sky.
Tell me how you feel.

Is it not a wonderful world?
Have you ever made a flower
That keeps bearing fruits?
Thank the wisdom of creation.

Look at the birds up high.
And think of your own self.
Then ask who you are.
You see, you are nobody.

Imagine how the clouds hang
And how you came to be among men:
Guess how to take death away.
How little is man.

We live in a wonderful world
With a wonderful creator.
The one living from ages to time indefinite:
His name is Jehovah.

## WHO CAN JUDGE MAN?

The sun shone all day,
The rain fell all night,
The wind blew harder and harder.
Until man began to cry in boredom.

Why too much sunshine all day?
Why this heavy rain?
The wind too much to bear,
The boredom too much to support.

But though these changes in climate,
The farmer welcomed the rain.
The builder was furious with the rain:
Who can judge man?

The time is suitable for me
But unsuitable for you.
You are to defend yourself in sageness
And confront the changes in climate.

## NO MAN IS PERFECT

No man is perfect.
Mistakes are on every man.
No man is above mistakes.
No man is perfect.

Do not criticize your fellow-man.
For you yourself are not perfect.
Why expect perfection?
You are apt to make a mistake.

No one was born perfect.
We all learned what we do.
As we can commit error in speech.
So can we die through error.

We are all fighting to perfection
But the way is too far to go.
Knowing that many books will not
Make you perfect, why daily criticise?

Do not force yourself not to err;
Correction is there for you.
Better to commit the errors than
To stay idle to avoid them.

Errors are never on purpose.
They're there because you did not know.
Education has no end;
Ask and you will know.

Better asking to know,
Than forcing to be perfect.
No one blames you for asking;
Ask and you will know.

## BE PATIENT, TIME WILL TELL

Be patient, time will tell.
Do not forward presents for privileges.
If you are apt.
Time will tell.

Do not force things out,
And do not pretend you know much.
The unlettered will be taken.
And you will be left pending.

Did you come to meet me?
Do not covet my seat:
I came before you came.
Be patient: time will tell.


## WHY WIDOWS?

Widows, widows. oh, poor widows.
What caused your widowhood?
Accident, war or sickness?
But remember it is always widows.

Always widows because the young girl,
For material sake, did not marry her equal.
She preferred the wealthy old man,
For better joy and happiness.

If you will suffer before reaping,
You will live to your end with your equal;
But your avidity leaves you with the
Opulent old man and soon you are left a widow.

9

## IF YOU WANT TO LIVE LONGER

If you want to live longer.
Obey the law.
If you want to be in peace.
Obey the law.
The law is there for your happiness.
Why not obey it?

But is the law against your faith?
And is your faith against the law?
What do you have against the law?
What has the law against you?

The law is made for you not for me.
The law is made for me not for you.
But whatever the case may be,
The law has to be obeyed or disobeyed for
Happiness or sadness.

Here is the law of God.
Here is the law of Children of God:
The promise of the law of God
Is Everlasting life.
What is the promise of the Law of
Children of God?

## THE SKY

How wonderful is the sky,
Hanging up quiet and slow.
How glorious is your silver,
Turning above a million heads.

Birds flying up high,
Under your treeless park
Which seems to them a playground,
Your blue covering invited them.

Underneath you, high mountains.
Underneath you, thick forest.
Underneath you, talcum flowers.
How high are your feet.

Wonderful, wonderful, wonderful.
A hanging cloud in your bosom.
From where falls the rain
And protects us from the ray-fury.

Bright moon at night,
Bright stars at dawn.
Sweet music early morning:
We shall always need you.

## LIFE HAS A VALUE

Life has a value
Which makes its possessors live.
Never attempt hanging yourself,
Never be bored in life.

Man without life is no man,
And creation without life is dead.
Keep fighting for life,
For it's more valuable than riches.

Gain all and lose your life,
What stupidity on your behalf.
Lose all and gain life,
The wisest course to choose.

Be happy with the life you have,
And never regret what you lost.
Your past can be reinstated,
Pray to have life always.

## POOR YOUNG VICTOR

Born the unique son of poor parents,
He was carefully taken care of.
Poor parents emptied their pockets
To look after him in school.

From Kindergarten to Primary,
Middle to Secondary,
Lower to Upper forms,
And finally entered university.

12

First year a success
For he studied his lessons well,
Which made his family proud
To have him for a son.

Victor went through his studies,
And out with flying colours he came,
The parents proud to be of aid,
But a tragedy and Victor lost his life.

## THE FOREST

There's a forest in a large continent,
Thick, thick and dark.
Walk under the Odum tree,
Enjoy the great forest treasure.

Hard to penetrate the forest,
But what a paradise amid the trunks;
With birds in rainbow chirping up high,
How great to be in the forest.

Left, right, east and west,
All surrounded by colourful trees.
Yes, beautiful tall trees
With their numerous sweet flowers.

Raise up your head,
And see the rays fighting through.
Yes, such a wonderful sight,
Why destroy the forest?

13

How green is the forest,
The Oak and the Onyina trees.
Giants and masters they are,
But humbly you may touch them.

Providing man's need,
How intelligent is its maker.
Thanks be to Him,
For God is great.

## OLD AGE

O wicked old age,
How worrisome you are,
Waiting for mankind at forty and fifty.
When do you quit the generation?

Man fighting for good health.
But meeting him at the harvest time.
How painful, how pitiless, how headstrong,
For making weak the experienced one?

Old age, old age, old age,
Why come so early in human life,
Becoming another obstacle for progress?
Oh, please, leave humans alone.

You have known the great ones,
You have known the experienced ones,
You have known the best of the era,
But the inexperienced youth you know not.

Man is tired of your generous service;
So please leave us alone.
You have already achieved your lot;
So, sir, it is time for you to leave.

## MARRIAGE

When I was a bachelor,
I thought marriage was honey
So I decided to enter into it.
But I soon realised my opposite thought.

When a bachelor, I was always alone.
I ate my palatable dish alone,
And went out for walks alone;
But this freedom I did not appreciate.

After my becoming two,
I shared my food with the one I loved,
Went out in that pair,
I thought of another person.

This handcuff I put upon my hand.
I soon felt deprived of something,
And replaced with another.
No more one, but two.

But later I got warmth
When my work reduced to zero.
With new souls around me,
How great to be a father.

My children called me papa,
And my wife called me darling.
Such unique privilege for marrying,
I am proud to be a father.

## SWEET WIND

Sweet wind, sweet wind, sweet wind,
For health, for energy, for life.
Wind sweet, wind sweet, wind sweet,
How indebted are we to you.

Serving for warning and destruction,
Serving for merciless purification.
Blowing dead leaves here and there,
Wind sweet, wind sweet, wind sweet.

Putting dust into limpid eyes,
Falling a whole roof of man.
Uprooting giant, solid trunks,
How mighty is your power.

Oh, yes, transparent thing,
Quiet blind old thing,
But your anger ferocious and killing;
Have mercy on us, we pray you.


## O DEATH, WHY?

A great enemy is among men,
Whose name man fears to utter.
His head being as a bone,
O death, O death, O death.

A great friend to the sick,
A great friend to the old,
A great friend to the young,
O death, why, why, why?

Why taking infants away?
Why taking husbands away?
Why taking fathers and mothers away?
Why taking wives, brothers and sisters away?

Humans need you no more,
Why not leave them alone?
Though you care less about our cries,
Remember your time is near, too.

## POVERTY IS A GREAT DISEASE

Poverty is a great disease,
That sends its possessors away,
Far from what could be imagined,
Far from what could be told.

The poor in need,
Fight'ng all the way to freedom;
But poverty seizing his throat,
Peoples' food making his mouth water.

The desire being great to procure,
But poverty with its commanding rod,
They regard the future with avidity
And keep waiting for chance.

Poverty doing great harm,
The poor having no solution.
The rich caring less about this,
Leaving the poor sleeping in hunger.

Why this poverty?
Why? Because I was born poor,
And you were born rich.
Please have pity and help the poor.

## THE DIVORCE

My comrade Kwasi entered into marriage;
He entered to relieve him from singleness.
The beginning was good and he mocked at me.
The middle was better and he expected good.
The third brought bad,
Yet he hoped for good.
The fourth brought worse,
He grimaced and still hoped for good;
But it was replaced with the worst and
So Kwasi, not being able to go further, resigned.

## THE MOON

Oh, look at the moon.
High up there in the sky:
Wonderful as it may be,
Leave all to nature.

Passing over the sea at night,
Swinging over the stream at dawn.
Giving its silvery glides,
Give all to nature.

Over there above the mountains,
Moving over the clouds.
Its freedom great in the sky,
Give all to nature.

Sending its light to man,
Bringing its glory to humans.
Peace as it is up high,
Give all to nature.

Its admiration perceived by all,
Its great service to man.
What man might have hung it high there?
Give all to nature.

Yes, give all to nature,
But nature came not by itself.
Surprising as this may be,
Its owner is Jehovah, thank Him.


## BE LIKE A CHILD


How innocent a child is,
Crying only when hungry,
Crying only when sick,
But smiling when satisfied.

How formidable is a child,
So flexible, so humble.
A fact to know,
For a child must be humble.

Be like a child,
And you will be the greatest.
Be like a child,
And you will succeed.

Do not wear the shoes of a beast,
And you will live long.
Do not wear the shoes of a beast,
For man is man not a beast.

## THE SEA

There is a great sea around me,
Front, back, East and West.
This mighty flow of water around me,
Who am I to command you?

Washing your shores as you like,
How white are your waves.
Working day and night freely,
How great is your mightiness.

Standing at the shore,
I saw the canoes dodging its blows.
Terrible as they were,
The sea authorised them to go.

O mighty supplier of salt,
You have served with great fidelity.
For ages you are great,
How mighty are your works.

Keeping fish in your forests,
Feeding them for man's good.
Keeping animals in your zoos,
How mighty are your works.

Go to the beach,
And see the holiday makers.
What do you think they are doing?
The sea is serving them.

Under a tall coconut tree,
I saw the glides building.
Breaking against the steep cliffs,
You are a mighty thing.

The wind blew,
The moon gave its light.
Over the waters at night,
How peaceful is the sea.

## BLACK AND WHITE

Black, black, black,
A great colour in the universe.
White, white, white,
A great colour in the universe.

Nothing like black,
Nothing like white.
Cherish the black,
Cherish the white.

Why condemning the black?
Why condemning the white?
Leave black and white alone,
For they complete world beauty.

No colour is above the other.
You are all one:
The same mother, the same father.
You are all one.

Don't misjudge your fellow-man.
No man has green blood.
Leave tales alone,
For all men are equal.

Leave enmity alone,
And stop dividing yourselves.
Love your neighbour as yourself,
And bring peace to all men.

Don't think because I am black.
I am not a brother;
Don't think because I am white,
I am not a sister.

We are all one.
Leave colour alone.
Seek for peace instead,
And make God happy.


## NIGHT


And the sun set and night grew.
Volail in their coop;
Man in his abode,
And the devil kept awake.

Ten million stars appeared.
And the moon shone.
Insufficient, says man,
And generates his electricity.

## THE GOOD QUALITIES

How gentle is the man?
She's a respectful lady.
An obedient child he is.
How humble are they?

They recommended him as meek.
Yes, she's kind.
It is true she's long suffering;
Follow the course of truthfulness.

A man may be good,
A woman may be patient,
But wherever lies self-control.
All goes well.

How rich is love
That brings peace to its possessors?
Jump for joy,
For faith is your saviour.

## THE USEFUL TREE

See the palm tree, a useful tree.
Branches for broom.
Branches for baskets,
Branches for fire, a useful tree.

Palm nuts for soup.
Palm nuts for oil,
Dried kernels for oil,
A useful tree.

Extracting palm wine,
A good wine.
Picking mushrooms.
Akokonno and Asommodwe*.

Building huts,
Covering huts.
Food for birds,
Food for squirrels.

Serving for light,
A source of energy.
Serving for soap,
Serving for cleanliness.

The beautiful straight palm tree,
Serves for its fame always.
Go to an African village,
And you will be told.

* *Akokonno* is a larva that later turns into *Asommodwe*, a kind of
beetle produced in the palm tree.

## THE AFRICAN WOMAN

The African woman,
A woman of women.
Getting up while it's yet right,
Going to bed late at night.

Carrying her baby on her back,
Carrying her pot of water from
The riverside.
Yet you find cassava on her head.

Going to the farm,
Bringing food.
Pounding fufu,
Eating gari and groundnut soup.

Not competing with her husband
Not deciding without him.
A full respect with humbleness,
Yes, African woman you are great.


## THE STOMACH

There's an object called stomach
Situated in mammals.
The most selfish of all creatures,
For he is never satisfied.

You feed him several times daily,
But he will never be satisfied.
He's always ungrateful,
And keeps man working to death.

25

You, O stomach,
Why do you torment humans so?
Feeding you with all the food in the world,
And rewarding rather with sickness.

Your anger, when not nourished,
Makes mammals boney.
When well fed,
You give them fat, a disease.

As long as you live,
Mammals will always feed you.
Do not often be troubled,
For mammals work for you.

## MOUNTAIN AFAJATO

There's an enormous land,
That has lifted itself up high,
Higher than all the lands,
Calling itself Afajato.

Tall trees upon its head,
Hard rocks upon its belly.
A flowing stream under its feet,
Oh, mountain you are beautiful.

In you, treasure.
Upon you, riches.
Upon your rocks, peace.
How huge are your arms.

We cannot compare you to anything,
You are mighty.
Having companions worldwide.
You are great.

## THE DAY

The sun rose,
And the day came.
Activities began.
Grace to the almighty.

Taking his axe, man went to
His farm.
Sweating before eating.
"What a punishment," he said.

## THE HEAVY RAIN

As I sat at my window,
I felt the blowing wind.
Going out to see,
My surprise, the dark clouds.

The wind blowing harder,
The trees dancing fast.
Dried leaves falling aplenty,
A new season begins.

Then came the drizzles,
Light at first,
Heavy at last,
And down the rain came pouring.

The forest received its share,
The gardens had theirs.
Full became the hungry river,
"Great welcome," said the frog.

Dirt gathered by leaves,
From cleaning the air,
Was washed away,
Some vegetation to feed as food.

Fruits were washed,
Ready to be eaten,
And the air was cleaned,
For life on the earth.

Habitation of some creatures
Was washed clean.
Water for cooking, water for bathing;
And, Oh, drinking water at last!

Yes, the wisdom of the Intelligent God,
Jehovah the Creator, has caused these,
Bringing prosperity to the good and the bad,
Who dares challenge His work?

The heavens thundered,
And lightning flashed with fear,
I went to bed to escape the rain-fury,
Awaking, the sky was blue, free from rain.

## UNITY IS A HELPER

It is true,
Unity is a tight knot;
The strength of two,
The way to success.

Are you separated?
Where are you going?
Only one, you will be miserable;
Return, unity is a helper.

Do you enjoy music,
Don't deceive yourself.
The good sound came not all alone,
Unity worked it out.

Why can't men be united,
And form one precious people?
If you are to find your own way,
A fall will welcome you.

Follow the wisest course,
Go together and
Success will smile at you.
Think again.

# THE MOST PRECIOUS BOOK

There's a book under the sun,
That contains hundreds of pages,
History, geography and prophecies,
Most precious book ever written.

The most precious book,
Written centuries ago,
Not through man's imperfection,
But by the heavenly Divine.

Yes, man has always printed the holy words,
But not man's ideology.
A book faithful and true,
A book of counsel and salvation.

From creation it has existed.
And yet a precious book it is.
Great men taking its wisdom,
The poor in its pages.

A precious book is among men
Solving all the difficulties men
Have created.
A book you, too, must possess.

Millions pass through it for wisdom,
Millions pass through it for salvation.
Men, women and children together,
What a precious book for mankind.

What book can be compared to you?
A book of knowledge and morality.
Giving hope and life to mankind,
A book to tell you why you live.

A precious book in a thousand languages,
In Twi, Ga and Ewe, too.
The most read book in the universe,
This book is the Bible.


## THIS WORLD


We live in a world full of problems.
Diffculties everywhere,
Peace out of contro'
And people always talking about you.

Yes, people will talk of you,
Get treasure, and people will talk of you.
Be poor, and people will talk of you.
Work or stay jobless and people will talk of you.
Dress or stay naked and people will talk of you.
Success or failure, and people will talk of you.
Grow fat, grow thin, and people will talk of you.
All you do, people will talk of you.

People will talk of you so will you listen to them?
It's your own business.
Listen to them and grow thorns on your head.

Listen to no man, and you will succeed.
Yes, all that you do, people will talk of you.
Turn away from them, and you will succeed.
Turn away from them, and you will live in peace.

## THESE LADIES

While in the body of the moving horse,
I looked and there my Lily.
My heart beating in my chest fast,
Stopping me to alight from the crying body.

The chill that followed fell over
My tender heart and had to see
The blossom that was all I am.
Descending further, a quick return made.

I stood afar full of happiness
To meet my dear lady in a pause.
Then came a strange man who consented to
Fetch me the palm I had been in need of.

But the man was shabby in his mode,
And smoke came from his nose.
His teeth grey and black
Sent my lady far away.

"Gentleman, gentleman," came the regretful voice.
Great excuse for making her go.
My appellation he sent to her.
But the quick return proved the worse.

She fixed her limpid eyes on me,
Which provoked my blood into running fast.
Then came another moving horse for her,
Leaving me in a total disgrace.

## DAUGHTER OF MAN

O daughter of man,
Once in the maternal covering,
Male or female the questions were.
But pot broken white are the teeth.

The sweet catlike voice,
The bright eyes that give way to happy tears.
The round face that has wonders ahead,
The many good things that never lacked.

She walks as palm tree, straight,
Where the beauty lies all alone.
The melodious smile that brightens the face,
How do you believe in the mortal soul?

At home under the maternal roof,
The paternal severity of her abode.
Nothing needing that is not provided,
Like the soil in its production.

Then come the matrimonial days,
Where the handsome debonair face, demure.
All night in the abundant dream,
Until her eyes grasped the bearded face.

"Where is he that my soul deserves?"
It says when they have met at last.
Staying under the shading flowers,
Where the blossom grows lovely and bright.

33

Three years the enemy circulates,
Putting his nose into the perfect union.
I hate this, I hate that.
And finally the string falls broken.

Then, said the pretty palm to her lord:
"When a child, father you obey,
When fruits are born to quit the maternal
Roof, Always obey husband as head."

Slavery this may be,
But a work of nature it is.
Crying for total liberty from the knot,
But granted uses not the power.

You have known submission for long;
Yes, it is the work of nature,
To make you and your family happy,
To bring happiness to your marriage.


## PEOPLE WILL LAUGH AT YOU

If you have experience in something,
And people know you are keen in
the experience but you go away from the
experience, people will laugh at you,
no matter who you are.

Kofi has walked for thirty years
but as he was hurrying away, he slipped
on a banana skin on his path;
People could not help and laughed at him.

## ALL MEN ARE EQUAL

All men are equal;
Equal are all men.
Two hands, ten toes,
Ten fingers, two legs.

Two eyes, two nostrils,
Two ears, two brows.

One mouth, one blood.
One creator, one earth.
All men, being equal,
Deserve equal rights.

## BE CAREFUL

Be careful in all you do;
Care, a word in itself
Is a protector of life.

Do not hurry in anything,
Take care and do it well, for
Carelessness is the beginning of
A lost soul.

Do you want to utter a word,
Do it with care.
For there's nothing like care.

You want an egg, *n 'est-ce pas ?*
Hold it with care,
Or it will fall and break.

Knowing the importance of care.
Cross your *t's* and dot your *i's*,
And all will go well.


## IT IS NEVER EASY TO DIE


It is never easy to die.
As the child dies,
So the old die.
It is never easy to die.

Do you think it is easy to die?
My friend, do not deceive yourself.
You suffer before you die;
It is never easy to die.

You may be sick,
You may be burnt,
You may be decapitated,
You may be drowned in the depths.

You die because of your imperfection,
Or there would be no death.
Do not lightly mention death.
For it is not easy to die.

No one knows how and when he will die,
You may die through an event.
Do not accuse God for not being good;
For you kill yourself.

There's no determined day for anyone.
If humans were perfect,
Man would live longer;
But you are not perfect and death is

Waiting for you. Death will never come
By itself; it always passes through some
Event. Take care of yourself,
For it is not easy to die.


## NO MAN WILL BE SATISFIED

No man will be satisfied,
Despite his great material possessions.
Having even the whole world in his house,
He will never be satisfied.

There's a reason for this,
For the poor also will never be satisfied.
Boredom satisfies only the lazy;
Yes, no man will be satisfied.

To be satisfied means to give up life.
Your desire and plans make you live,
Enjoying a longer life on earth;
No man will be satisfied.

37

Do not have a wicked desire
To gain wealth through evil.
Be happy with what you have,
And you will enjoy life fully.

You may prosper today,
And fall the next.
Pursue your course slowly,
But know you will never be satisfied.

## WHAT HAVE YOU LEARNED TODAY?

What have you known today?
When you see the sun rise,
And then see it set,
Know that a day has gone by.

Did it slip away freely?
Have you learned something new?
What new thing have you learned?
You yourself know.

Never let the sun set
Without learning anything new.
Every day bringing something new,
What have you learnt today?

## DO NOT THINK YOURSELF GREAT

Do not think yourself great.
Do not think yourself "big."
There's someone elsewhere greater,
There's someone elsewhere "biggest."

Humble yourself,
Live equally with all men.
Avoiding pride,
Keep your dignity.

## PEACE IS NATURE

Peace is nature,
And nature's peace.
Do you really need peace?
Peace is in nature.

No man can bring peace
Without first asking nature.
Study the rules of nature,
And you will achieve peace.

Shut the door on pollution
And close the door on spoiling the earth.
Opening your heart to nature,
You will know its peace.

You create your own problems
And no way to appease them.
Go back to the original peace,
And you will know the peace in nature.

## IT IS TOO MUCH FOR ME

It is too much for me,
With my nine children and a wife.
Such a task not being easy
While my dear wife was alive.

But the flower soon closed,
And I was left with the eight and one
Children;
We have dearly loved.

She bade me farewell, adieu.
And went on her bitter journey,
A journey I did not authorise,
But had to consent to let her go.

Oh, she has left me alone,
To swim in this unfaithful world alone.
How do I get her back,
She is gone for good.

Oh, it is a pity,
To lose my dear wife,
Now that she is gone forever,
What of the children she has left me.

I shall never try again,
But already it is too late.
Who can call her back for me
To help the children grow?

## I HAVE A BLACK CAT

I have a black cat,
Whose name is Avril;
Young as she is,
She tries her tricks on me.

She caressed my foot one day,
And ran away in hiding.
I chased her up at speed,
And found her behind the door.

Again she ran past the kitchen door,
Pretending going to the chamber.
But she returned to the kitchen again,
Thinking I did not notice her.

I went to the kitchen at last,
And saw her flat on the floor.
Seeing I have a better brain than hers,
She never played tricks on me again.

## FIND OUT FOR ME

No one looked back
When the dead were buried
In the heart of the dark forest
That May sunset.

Man is nothing.
He was not left on the earth,
He was buried in the earth,
To continue his journey alone.

And his place was taken,
And his work was forgotten;
Why was he born?
I do not know.

If you are born to live,
Why should you die?
If you are born to die,
Why should you be born?

Find out for me.
I will give all to know;
I want to live.
Find out for me.

## DO NOT WAIT TO HEAR YOU ARE GOOD

Do not wait to hear you are good.
Prove yourself good to all.
Partiality everywhere,
Prove yourself good to all.

Prove yourself good to all,
Acquire knowledge and give love.
Do not wait to hear you are good;
Your judgement is in their heart.

"Am I good?"
You know it yourself.
Go deep into your heart,
And you will find the answer.

Do not wait to hear you are good,
You only know what is in your heart.
Prove yourself good to all,
Do not wait to hear you are good.

Your heart is your face,
And your face is your judge.
Remove evil from your physiognomy,
Do not wait to hear you are good.

## THE GRAVE ASKS NO BILL

The grave asks no bill,
Receiving the rich and the poor,
None pay rent.

Do you want to purchase something?
Do not go to the grave,
For the grave has nothing to offer you.
You will only turn to dust.

Do you want to see your dead?
Do not go to the grave,
For they are not there,
Only the sad end of humans.

Do not listen to tales,
No one has returned from the grave.
Be careful of myths, for they will
Only break your heart.

You die and you die.
All you give to the dead,
You give to the termites.
Think of yourself and leave the dead alone.

The evil spirit presents itself,
Do not think it is your brother,
Why run away?
The devil is chasing me.

Be happy with the life you have
And forget the enemy tomb.
For you only become food,
For the rats.

## I WILL FORGET

I will forget;
Take time to explain,
Or I will forget.

Do not ask me to read
Repeat it to me,
Or I will forget.

Be patient with me:
Do not force me to learn,
Or I will forget.

I do not want to forget;
Give me the understanding,
Or I will forget.

Let me be in need;
And teach me what I want to know,
And I will not forget.

## DO NOT BE ANNOYED WITH ME

Do not be annoyed with me,
I am your brother.
Do not be annoyed with me,
I am your sister.

Do not be annoyed with me,
I am your wife.
Do not be annoyed with me,
I am your husband.

You know how I love you.
You know how we have been.
If today I offend you,
Do not be annoyed with me.

I did not know,
And I am still learning.
If today I offend you,
Do not be annoyed with me.

## TELL ME MY MISTAKES

Tell me my mistakes,
And I will correct them.
Tell me my mistakes.
And I will thank you.

Do not hesitate.
And leave me mistaken.
I also need correction. for
I am a human being like you.

It is never easy to climb.
Teach me the way.
Tell me my mistakes,
And I will praise you.


## I WILL RESPECT

I will respect,
I do not know who you are.
But I will respect.

I will not select who to respect,
For the sake of respect,
I will respect.

I will respect an honourable person,
I will respect a poor fellow,
Who knows if it is an angel disguised?

47

I will not be selective with my respect,
Everyone is a fellow human,
So I will respect.

Even if you are nobody,
I am nobody too,
So I will respect.

## PEOPLE ARE WATCHING YOU

People are watching you.
Turn your back,
You will see nobody,
But people are watching you.

Are you concealing yourself?
You only deceive your soul.
How can you hide yourself?
People are watching you.

Close your door,
And hide in a box.
Do you think no one is watching you?
God is watching you.

All that you do,
People are watching you.
The evil in your heart is on your face,
So people are reading you.

Do good,
Open your heart,
Do not hide any evil,
For people are watching you.

People are watching you.
Behave well,
Throw away evil,
For people are watching you.

To escape all troubles.
Do good in light,
Do not hide in darkness,
For people are watching you.

## STOP SELLING THE EARTH

**W**hy sell the earth?
Oh, selfish humans of our time,
Greedy as you may be,
You keep selling the free gift of God.

Water is a gift, and you sell it.
Food is a gift, and you sell it.
Help is a gift, and you sell it.
Oh man, what is wrong with you?

You pay before you sleep.
You pay before "nature's call,"
You pay before justice.
Oh man, what is wrong with you?

There's suffering,
Because you sell the free gift
Of God. There's poverty because
You sell what has been given free.

You have prevented your fellow-man
To share the same gift,
And have acquired all for yourself.
Oh man, what is wrong with you?

## I WILL ALWAYS SPEAK MY MIND

I will always speak my mind,
I will not be a doll
And gape at people;
I will always speak my mind.

I have fine thick lips,
That enable me to speak out,
Even if I am dumb;
I will always speak my mind.

Speaking my mind everyday.
And helping my brothers to maturity,
A thing I shall never cease to do;
I will always speak my mind.

I will always speak my mind,
I will search from my skull,
And find the bread and butter
To feed my fellow humans.

But if I am quiet
Do not think I am a fool.
I just do not want to talk;
I can always speak my mind.

When you insult me,
And I do not retaliate,
Do not think I am deaf;
I can always speak my mind.

Poverty makes me hold my tongue,
And obey the wealthy one.
There lies my handicap, yet,
I can always speak my mind.

Do not look down upon me,
And think me stupid.
I have passed through that stage;
And I can always speak my mind.

Curse be on poverty,
That has imprisoned my mouth.
Do not think me weak;
For I can always speak my mind.

## I WILL ALWAYS SMILE

I will always smile,
For I also am a human being,
What prevents me from smiling?
I will always smile.

I will not see the twilight
Without first smiling.
Or I will be called no man.
I will always smile.

I will not be excessive
And close the glory of my face,
Or fellow humans will hide from me.
I will always smile.

I will smile a little every day,
And bring my heart to my face.
Sincere as this may be;
I will always smile.

I will gain nothing but hatred,
If I do not smile.
I will become an object of talk,
So I will always smile.

I will always smile,
And gain the fruit of the spirit.
To gain the favour of my foes,
I will always smile.

Yes, smiling is part of my daily bread.
It is for you, too.
Do not stay without a smile,
Let us smile now.

## BE CONTENT WITH WHAT YOU HAVE

Be content with what you have,
And what you are.
Do not think of what I have,
And what I am.

## TO THE LAND OF PERFECTION

He started his journey early,
To the land of perfection.
But crooked was the path,
He never reached perfection.

He had a good diet,
And had the best of life.
Comfortable as those were,
He never reached perfection.

He often fell sick,
And often heard of death.
Thinking himself favoured to live,
He never reached perfection.

A great man he became,
And great money he pocketed.
Happy and unhappy as he was,
He never reached perfection.

Then he felt pains in his body,
And gradually began to die.
Improbable as it was for him,
He never reached perfection.

He was sent suddenly home,
Where he lost his great fortune.
Even losing his young wife,
He never reached perfection.

Great doctors were called,
Best medicines were applied.
But soon gave way to death,
He never reached perfection.

## BE CAREFUL, NO TRIAL DEATH

Be careful, no trial death;
You die only once
And you never come back again.
Be careful, no trial death.

Do not think it is an off-day,
And drink to inebriation.
If you really love life;
Be careful, no trial death.

Do your best,
And pray for long life.
Living to please God and man,
Be careful, no trial death.

## A WOMAN AMONG MEN

There's a woman among men,
Who comports like a woman,
All actions calm and slow,
Be a man.

A woman is flexible and weak,
Her arms seem a web.
A woman is frightful and puerile,
Be a man.

Are you not a man?
You are a man
In the skirt of a woman.
Be a man.

Go among men,
And show your man-power.
Do not be a woman,
Be a man.

You have cried before the blow,
You have wept before the death.
There's no need to cry when the head
Is already chopped off. Be a man.

You are among men,
You are a man,
Do not behave like a woman.
Be a man.

## DO NOT HINDER MY PROGRESS

Do not hinder my progress,
I am a human being like you.
Because I am under you,
You profit to step down on me?

Do not maltreat me,
And think I do not suffer.
You torment my soul;
Please do not hinder my progress.

If it were you,
You would have cried out.
I have a mouth, but I look with my eyes.
So please, do not hinder my progress,

I must eat, too.
I must enjoy, too.
If, for the moment I am under you,
Please do not hinder my progress.

## TELL THE LIE AND YOU ARE FREED

The more you humble yourself,
The more you are termed stupid.
O world of man,
When will you understand?
You tell the truth,
And you are taken to be foolish;
Tell the lie, and you are honoured.
Oh yes, mankind has gone wrong.
Please find out for me.
I cannot believe it;
It is too bad to be true;
But it is real.
You tell the lie, and you are set free.
You tell the lie, and it becomes money.
Oh wrong, wrong. It is wrong.
Till when will it continue?
Please find out for me.

## AN UNBALANCED WORLD

The world is shaking, shaking, shaking.
The world is shaking.
War in the north,
Tremors in the south.

The world is shaking, shaking, shaking,
The world is shaking.
Misunderstanding in the east,
Flood in the west.

The world is shaking, shaking, shaking,
The world is shaking.
Negotiations at the top,
Famine at the bottom.

The world is shaking, shaking, shaking,
The world is shaking.
It is unbalanced
It is unstable.

Hold fast.
Stand firm.
And keep from shaking in a
World without balance.


## GOD EXISTS


Do you take man for God?
I am not in harmony with you.
No man can be compared to God.
No animal can be compared to man.

Does God really exist?
That is a funny question.
Look over your shoulder;
What do you see?

Did you make what you see?
God is not man, God is God.
Reason well.
God exists.

You ask who is God?
Good.
He is the supreme spirit.
The maker of Heaven and earth.

He is the supreme being.
The Omnipotent,
The Creator and ruler of the Universe;
The Everlasting father.

God created you and me.
Do not try to see Him before believing in Him.
He is your heavenly father
Whose glory supersedes the sun.

God is the most High,
His unique name is Jehovah,
Under whose permission you live;
Thanks for His love.

## AMA, THE BLACK GIRL

A black girl has been born,
Yes, a very beautiful black girl has been born.
Born with indispensable beauty,
Born with riches in beauty.

She is my own sister, the second,
She is black, slim and strong,
In fact, she's pretty and gay.
Yes, a black girl has been born.

White eyes in a black body,
White teeth in a black skin.
Black hair, black lashes,
Yes, a black girl has been born.

Her bright, black complexion,
To compare to a black diamond.
Oh, beautiful girl, black girl,
Yes, a black girl has been born.

## MUSIC IN THE SKY

There's music in the sky,
And music in the trees.
Music in the air,
And music in the instrument.

Sweet, melodious music,
Running from nature's bosom,
Like cool water on your body,
Go to music.

## NATURE'S BEAUTY

There is nothing like a natural beauty.
Beauty in nature,
Beauty in creation;
Thank you, durable beauty.

Beauty in invention,
Beauty in construction.
They are artificial beauty;
Perishable beauty invented.

## LIZARD ON THE WALL

Once I saw a lizard on a wall,
Red head and a long tail.
I wondered what it was doing there,
But since it did not understand my language,
I could not pose him any question.

I stood aside, head in palm,
And gazed at the little creature.
As it began *packing* some ants on the wall
Another lizard came;
It was madame redhead.

As they were sharing the poor ants
Other lizards, seeing what was happening,
Also joined the banquet.
But when they were ready to leave,
Some boys who understood their language came and,
Killing all the lizards around,
They left madame redhead.
Then, asking why such an evil act,
They told me the dead lizards were not invited.

## MAN AND PROBLEMS

The abundance of food on the earth
Is as the grass germinating
On the banks of the Volta near Adomi.
Crabs eating to their satisfaction
And fishes to their brims with great joy

On land, multitudes of creatures.
Animals eating in praise of their maker,
Birds pecking in the happiness of their freedom,
Amphibians roaming in their liberty;
But man groaning in deep agony and dismay.

Why this problem with man,
And why individual problems?
How to solve them?
And when will they disappear from the soil
Which is condemned to destruction.

Man has gone, and even to the moon,
Man has gone, and even deep into science,
Man has gone, and even developed countries,
Man has gone, and even advanced in all;
Man has gone, and yet has nothing to eat.

Difficulties are everywhere,
With great consequences falling to all.
Hunger touching and slimming beautiful souls,
Thirst in the depths and showing the hunger bone,
With death reducing dilemmas in eternal sadness.

The rich king suffers sleepless nights,
The partial judge commits everlasting injustice,
The evil-doer pitiless in his non-stop crimes,
Faithful sinners in their great sins;
With the poor peasant getting always poorer.

Why are there closing boundaries for fellow humans,
Why inequality on the free earth?
Why is there selfishness, corruption and infidelity all
        around;
Why maltreat the suffering handicapped?
Why talk about problems without solution?

Oh yes, I do now remember
The answer to the multiple problems,
The forgotten, supreme wisdom;
God the father almighty.
Why not go to Him?

He has promised a joyful paradise,
Where problems will be no more.
He is the creator.
Wake up, for it is time
To lay problems in His hands for their solution.

## LADIES AND GENTLEMEN

Ladies and Gentlemen,
I have a word for you.
Come nearer to me,
And lend me your ears.

You are in a world
Where it is hard to live.
Do battle upon battle to live,
Still carry your armour.

Do not approach any man with confidence,
And do not always depend upon a promise.
Failure will break your heart,
And great will your regret be.

It is not easy to succeed.
You will fail and will succeed;
But be calm when you fail,
And wait for a good time to come.

The world is round,
Round as the sun, round as the moon.
Glance around and see its work,
And round will be your mouth.

But keep patient
And look for a crab's hole;
If you put your hand into a cobra's hole
It will bite you to death.

## YOU WORK FOR YOUR FELLOW-BEING

You work for your fellow-being,
Day and night, night and day.
All you do on this globe,
You do for your fellow-being.

Go to the farm,
Build a house,
Open a big factory,
And you work for your fellow-being.

Hunt at night,
Sell in the market,
Sing and dance,
And you work for your fellow-being.

Are you a doctor?
Are you a specialist?
Are you a teacher?
You only work for your fellow-being.

Have love for all
And throw laziness away.
Do what you do with all your might,
For you work for your fellow-being.

## THE WORLD CHANGES

Do not think you will always wear
The same coat.
The world is changing fast
And tomorrow you will wear a tattered cloak.

Do not think you will always have
The same wealth.
The world is changing fast
And tomorrow you will beg for bread.

The poor may rejoice
And the rich may lament.
The world is changing fast.
Waiting for tomorrow, you will understand.

## BE HUMBLE

I am torturing, torturing, torturing.
The sun is aware,
The moon is aware.
Be humble.

The wind blew, blew, blew.
The lights saw me,
The torture continued,
Be humble.

The load was borne.
The torture lessened,
The sky smiled,
Be humble.

Be humble, humble, humble.
Be humble and be great,
Be humble and be cherished,
Be humble.

## IMPOSSIBLE BUT TRUE

While couples bring forth for happiness,
The medicine man fights for their lives.
The soldier training to kill them all,
Oh, dear, find out for me.

## BEAUTIFUL PEOPLE

There are becutiful people on the earth.
Babies, children, young and old,
Jumping and playing here and there,
Travelling and meeting friends from afar.

Beautiful people on the islands,
Beautiful people on the deserts.
Playing varieties of games in joy,
Swimming in rivers, in the seas.

West and East with beautiful blacks,
The North with African whites,
In the South a mixture of people,
Golden on the islands.

Going to Europe, all beautiful whites.
Red and yellow people in Asian parts.
America in a pure rainbow.
Oh, people, you are beautiful.

Some short, some tall,
Some fat and some thin.
Beautiful as this may be,
Oh, people you are beautiful.

Oh, people you are beautiful.
Hair in colours over women,
Beautiful souls with nothing to compare to
them.
Oh, how beautiful it is to live.

People in colours around the earth,
Completing the beauty of flowers and all.
Beautiful, beautiful, repeating again,
How proud I am to be one of you.


## MONEY

You work for money
And money works for you.
You overwork for money
And money overworks you.

You take care of money,
And money takes care of you.
You misuse money,
And money misuses you.

## THE GREAT SCIENTIST OF NATURE

Look at the blue sky
And the colourless sea;
The colourless wind,
Forming a formidable sight.

But I saw the sea blue,
And coming to the surface,
I saw the wind too blue.
It is true, the blue sky reflected them.

And I went to the riverside,
And saw the river green.
True as these may be,
The tree green reflected them.

Oh, what a scientist,
A great scientist, indeed is above;
Whose brain goes up higher than man's;
His thoughts high to heaven.

## THIRD WORLD?

Why do you call me "Third World"?
It is not an honourable name.
It is not a deserving name,
By any human being.

Why do you call me "Third World"?
Am I not a human being, too?
Even if I do not have what you have,
Don't I need to be respected, too?

Why do you call me "Third World"?
You abuse my human right.
Just because I am not like you;
You break my heart.

The poor have problems,
The rich have problems, too.
The poor grow old,  the rich grow old, too.
All fall ill and all die, too.

Why do you call me: "Third World"?
Do not insult me for a little help.
I am a human being like you,
And have feelings like yours, too.

Why do you look down on me,
And call me "Third World"?
Is it not only one world?
Please, do not call me "Third World".

If you love me,
You will call me by my name.
Why call me names?
A name is better than riches.

Leave "Third World" alone.
Call me by my name,
Don't call me "Third World",
Call me by my name.

## WHO IS JESUS CHRIST?

The arch-angel son of God,
Transferred from Heaven,
To be born on the earth,
He was the greatest man who ever lived.

He was like Jehovah, his father,
Powerful but humble,
As appointed King of God, he died.
To redeem mankind from sin and death.

He loves humans, just as God does,
And wept when Lazarus died;
But he brought Lazarus back to life,
And healed the sick and the handicapped.

As King of Kings,
Jesus' throne is in heaven,
Where he is now as a spirit,
To rule and bring humans back to perfection.

73

He will rule forever as king,
And will solve all the earth's problems,
The dead will rise, and wars will cease,
Satan and his wicked angels destroyed.

He has been given authority,
Both in heaven and earth,
By God to rule as king, to accomplish,
God's Purpose: turn the earth into paradise.

Upon his victory in Heaven,
Over the rebellious demons,
Jesus, the mighty warrior,
Prepares his final war at Harmagedon.

Follow his footsteps that lead to God,
Put faith in his commandments,
Let the world know God's purpose for the earth,
And eternal life will be yours.